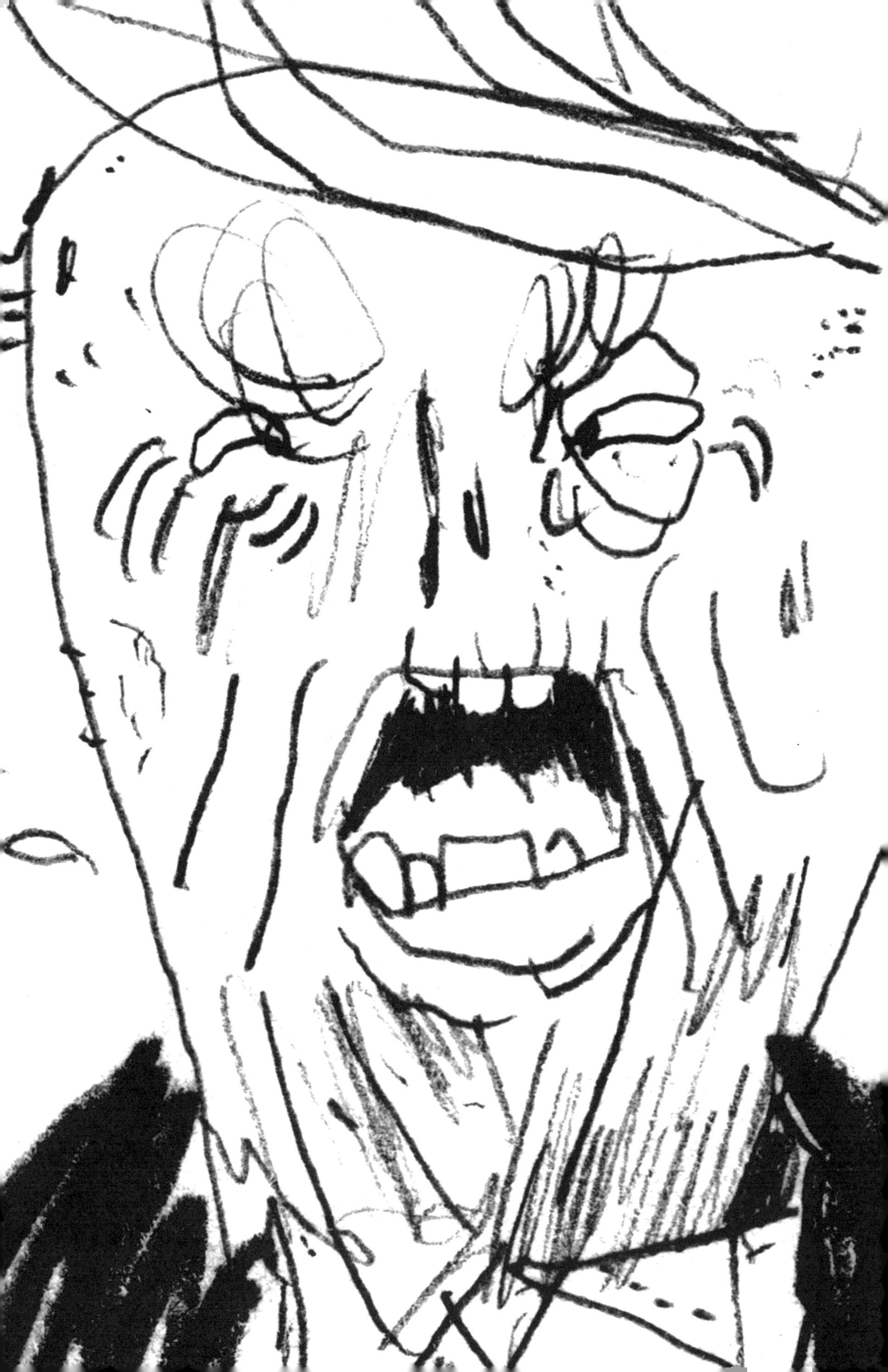

TRUMPTRUMP

volume 1: nomination to inauguration

JULY 21, 2016 - JANUARY 20, 2017

WARREN CRAGHEAD III

RETROFIT COMICS
BIG PLANET COMICS

For A.W., V.C.-W. and G.C.-W.
I'm sorry we let this happen.

TRUMPTRUMP vol. 1 is ©2017 Warren Craghead

This work originally published at trumptrump.biz
More at craghead.com

Thanks to B.B., J.S. and E.W.

Retrofit 68

ISBN 978-1-940398-71-6

Published by Retrofit Comics & Big Planet Comics
Philadelphia /// Washington, D.C.
retrofitcomics.com /// bigplanetcomics.com

Printed in Canada

I began drawing daily grotesque portraits of Donald J. Trump on July 21, 2016, the day he accepted the Republican nomination for president. Based on my earlier drawing projects, LADYH8RS and USAH8RS, I wanted to point at him, give succor to his enemies and make his supporters uncomfortable by reminding them that he is not a good person. I added quotes from Trump, and in the back of this book is an index of the sources.

I expected to be done on November 8, Election Day. Over the prior week I had Trump slowly melt into a puddle of goo. My plan after he was defeated was to keep drawing the puddle for a week, showing animals lapping at his liquefied carcass.

When he won, I vowed to keep drawing him "until this nightmare ends," as it says on the website where I share the drawings. I've been drawing him every day since, documenting what he and his minions and handlers have been doing.

This project started as mean yet otherwise straightforward caricatures. But as the weeks passed and I drew Trump more and more, he turned more gross and vile, emerging after the election as a kind of worm with a cloaca. His minions joined — Bannon, Sessions and Pence — and as Inauguration Day approached, the drawings became more detailed and angry, set in a burning and blasted-out landscape.

I've been inspired by (and stolen from) many artists in these drawings: Goya, Picasso, Steinberg, Kollwitz, Grosz — but especially Philip Guston and the wonderfully horrible drawings he made of the Nixon administration. My thanks, and apologies, to those artists. Thanks also to Box Brown of Retrofit Comics and Jared Smith of Big Planet Comics for encouraging and publishing this collection.

This book encompasses the first six months of drawings, which have continued. See them daily at trumptrump.biz.

Hopefully I can stop drawing this monster soon.

— Warren Craghead III, July 2017

"My IQ is one of the highest — and you all know it! Please don't feel so stupid or insecure; it's not your fault."

Trump accepted the Republican nomination for president on this day at the Republican National Convention

"They're bringing drugs, they're bringing crime, they're rapists"

Trump is referring to undocumented immigrants from Mexico.

"I know words, I have the best words... but there is no better word than 'stupid.'
Right?"

"I've said if Ivanka weren't my daughter, perhaps I'd be dating her."

"I'll stand up for Article Two, Article 12, you name it, of the Constitution."

"My fingers are long and beautiful, as, it has been well documented, are various other parts of my body."

Since the 1980s some have believed that Trump's hands are unnaturally small.

"Torture works, OK folks? ...Believe me, it works. ...Waterboarding is your minor form. Some people say it's not actually torture. Let's assume it is. But they asked me the question. What do you think of waterboarding? Absolutely fine. But we should go much stronger than waterboarding. That's the way I feel."

"I think the only difference between me and the other candidates is that I'm more honest and my women are more beautiful."

"You could see there was blood coming out of her eyes, blood coming out of her, 'wherever.'"

Trump's comment after a combative interview with Fox News' Megyn Kelly.

"I've got black accountants at Trump Castle and at Trump Plaza — black guys counting my money!... I hate it. The only kind of people I want counting my money are short guys that wear yarmulkes every day. Those are the kind of people I want counting my money. Nobody else. ... Besides that, I've got to tell you something else. I think that the guy is lazy. And it's probably not his fault because laziness is a trait in blacks. It really is; I believe that. It's not anything they can control."

"He's a Mexican. We're building a wall between here and Mexico."

Trump is referring to the ethnicity of Judge Gonzalo Curiel, who was overseeing a fraud lawsuit related to his Trump University. Curiel is Mexican-American.

"I could stand in the middle of Fifth Avenue and shoot people and I wouldn't lose voters…"

"I will build a great wall — and nobody builds walls better than me, believe me —and I'll build them very inexpensively."

"The problem is we have the Geneva Conventions, all sorts of rules and regulations, so the soldiers are afraid to fight... We can't waterboard, but they can chop off heads... I think we've got to make some changes, some adjustments."

"Political correctness is deadly."

"He's not a war hero. He is a war hero because he was captured. I like people who weren't captured."

Referring to Senator John McCain. Senator McCain was a held as a prisoner of war in the American-Vietnam War for over five years and suffered torture that left him with lifelong physical disabilities.

"I have so many websites, I have them all over the place. I hire people, they do a website. It costs me $3."

"I mean, I won't do anything to take care of [my children]. I'll supply funds and she'll take care of the kids. It's not like I'm gonna be walking the kids down Central Park..."

At a campaign rally where a supporter's baby was crying:
"I love babies. I hear that baby cry, I like it. What a baby. What a beautiful baby. Don't worry, don't worry. The mom's running around, like, don't worry about it, you know. It's young and beautiful and healthy and that's what we want."

A few minutes later:
"Actually, I was only kidding, you can get the baby out of here. I think she really believed me that I love having a baby crying while I'm speaking. That's OK. People don't understand. That's OK."

"Why can't we use nuclear weapons?"

"I think these polls — I don't know — there's something about these polls, there's something phony."

"If she gets to pick her judges, nothing you can do, folks. Although the Second Amendment people, maybe there is, I don't know."

Referring to his presidential rival Hillary Clinton and the amendment to the Constitution that many believe guarantees a right to bear arms.

"If you look at his wife, she was standing there. She had nothing to say. She probably — maybe she wasn't allowed to have anything to say. You tell me."

Trump talking about Khizr and Ghazala Khan, who spoke at the Democratic National Convention.

"I am now listening to people that are telling me to be easier, nicer, be softer. And you know, that's OK, and I'm doing that... Personally, I don't know if that's what the country wants."

"In fact, in many respects, you know they honor president Obama. ISIS is honoring President Obama. He is the founder of ISIS. He's the founder of ISIS, OK? He's the founder. He founded ISIS."

"I think I've made a lot of sacrifices. I work very, very hard. I've created thousands and thousands of jobs, tens of thousands of jobs, built great structures. I've had tremendous success. I think I've done a lot."

"There's a lot of women out there that demand that the husband act like the wife and you know there's a lot of husbands that listen to that..."

"Happy #CincoDeMayo! The best taco bowls are made in Trump Tower Grill. I love Hispanics!"

"...call up all of those countries... and say, 'Fellas you haven't paid for years, give us the money or get the hell out.' I'd say you've gotta pay us or get out. You're out, out, out... Maybe NATO will dissolve, and that's OK, not the worst thing in the world."

"I'm afraid the election is going to be rigged, I have to be honest."

"When you get these terrorists, you have to take out their families. They care about their lives, don't kid yourself. When they say they don't care about their lives, you have to take out their families."

"I don't know that we need to get out the vote. I think people that really want to vote, they're gonna just get up and vote for Trump. And we're going to make America great again."

"We're going to watch Pennsylvania. Go down to certain areas and watch and study make sure other people don't come in and vote five times."

"We have to protect our Second Amendment, which is under siege. Remember that: It's under siege."

"You know, it really doesn't matter what [the media] write as long as you've got a young and beautiful piece of ass."

"The beauty of me is that I'm very rich."

"He referred to my hands, if they're small, something else must be small. I guarantee you there's no problem. I guarantee it."

"We won with poorly educated. I love the poorly educated."

"Trump Steaks, where are the steaks? Do we have steaks?
We have Trump Steaks."

"All of the women on 'The Apprentice' flirted with me – consciously or unconsciously. That's to be expected."

"I don't think I've made mistakes. Every time somebody said I made a mistake, they do the polls and my numbers go up, so I guess I haven't made any mistakes."

"I will be the greatest jobs president that God ever created."

"I have a great relationship with the blacks."

"I will build a great, great wall on our southern border, and I will make Mexico pay for that wall. Mark my words."

"There may be somebody with tomatoes in the audience. If you see somebody getting ready to throw a tomato, knock the crap out of them, would you? Seriously. OK? Just knock the hell – I promise you, I will pay for the legal fees."

"I've had a beautiful, I've had a flawless campaign. You'll be writing books about this campaign."

"If Hillary Clinton can't satisfy her husband what makes her think she can satisfy America."

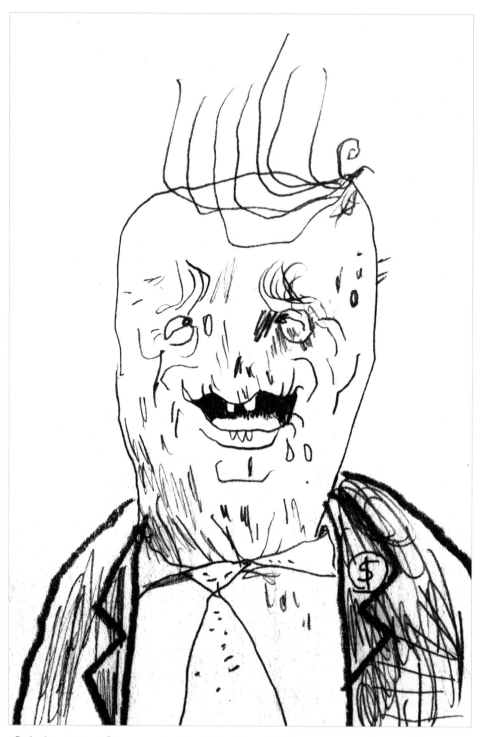

"[Vladimir Putin] is not going into Ukraine, OK, just so you understand. He's not gonna go into Ukraine, all right? You can mark it down. You can put it down."

Putin ordered the Russian military to invade Ukraine's territory of the Crimea in February 2014 and then supported rebels in eastern Ukraine with supplies and Russian soldiers.

"My whole life is about winning. I don't lose often. I almost never lose."

"Sadly, the overwhelming amount of violent crime in our major cities is committed by blacks and hispanics – a tough subject – must be discussed."

"I have a very substantial chance of winning. Make America great again. We're going to make America great again. I have a substantial chance of winning."

"We're losing our jobs like we're a bunch of babies."

"I think when he [Putin] calls me brilliant, I'll take the compliment, OK?"

"You know, it used to be to the victor belong the spoils. Now, there was no victor there, believe me. There was no victor. But I always said, 'Take the oil.'"

Trump speaking about the Iraq War

"26,000 unreported sexual assaults in the military – only 238 convictions. What did these geniuses expect when they put men & women together?"

"I think I would have a very, very good relationship with Putin. And I think I would have a very, very good relationship with Russia... He does have an 82% approval rating..."

"If [Putin] says great things about me, I'm going to say great things about him.
I've already said, he is really very much of a leader. I mean, you can say, oh, isn't
that a terrible thing – the man has very strong control over a country."

"Go back to Univision."

Trump to reporter Jorge Ràmos during a campaign event. Ramos questioned Trump's plan for a wall along the Mexican/U.S. border.

"Our leaders are stupid. Our politicians are stupid. And the Mexican government is much smarter, much sharper, much more cunning and they send the bad ones over because they don't want to pay for them."

"Watch and study the mosques, because a lot of talk is going on at the mosques."

"I think that her bodyguards should drop all weapons. I think they should disarm. Immediately. Let's see what happens to her. Take their guns away, OK. It'll be very dangerous."

About presidential rival Hillary Clinton

"We can't destroy the competitiveness of our factories in order to prepare for nonexistent global warming. China is thrilled with us!"

"Who knows about Obama? ...Who knows, who knows? Who cares right now? ...I have my own theory on Obama. Someday I will write a book, I will do another book, and it will do very successfully."

Trump launched himself onto the politcal scene as a strong and vocal "Birther,' questioning, with no evidence, whether President Obama's birth certificate was faked.

"This very expensive GLOBAL WARMING bullshit has got to stop."

"The point is that you can't be too greedy."

"Owning a great golf course gives you great power."

"I would do stop-and-frisk, I think you have to."

"I think Viagra is wonderful if you need it, if you have medical issues, if you've had surgery. I've just never needed it. Frankly, I wouldn't mind if there were an anti-Viagra, something with the opposite effect. I'm not bragging. I'm just lucky. I don't need it. I've always said, 'If you need Viagra, you're probably with the wrong girl.'"

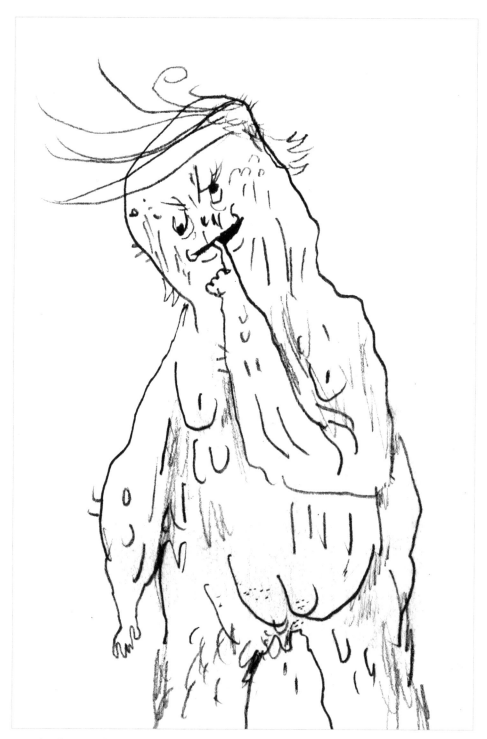

"Yeah, she's really something, and what a beauty, that one. If I weren't happily married and, ya know, her father…"

About his daughter, Ivanka

"I'm speaking with myself, No. 1, because I have a very good brain and I've said a lot of things. ...My primary consultant is myself."

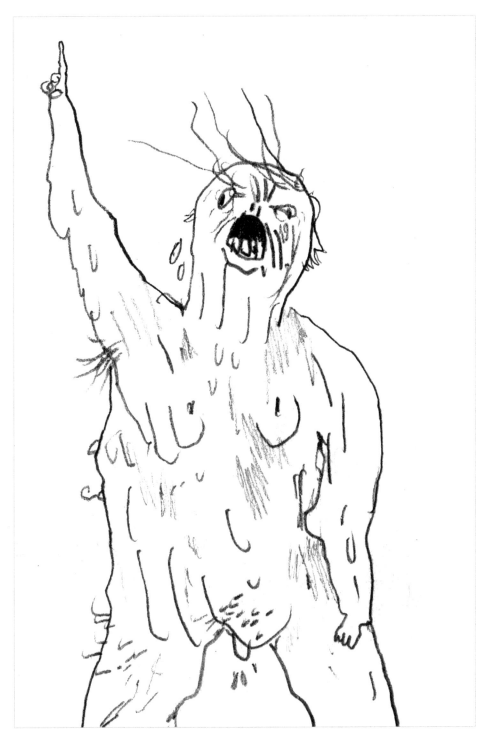

"'How are Mr. Trump's hands?' My hands are fine. You know, my hands are normal. Slightly large, actually. In fact, I buy a slightly smaller than large glove, OK?"

"A person who is very flat chested is very hard to be a 10."

"Let me tell you, I'm a really smart guy."

"I do whine because I want to win, and I'm not happy about not winning, and I am a whiner, and I keep whining and whining until I win."

"Just so you understand, I don't know anything about David Duke, OK?
I don't know anything about what you're even talking about with white
supremacy or white supremacists. So I don't know. I don't know – did he
endorse me, or what's going on? Because I know nothing about David Duke;
I know nothing about white supremacists."

*David Duke is an American white nationalist, politician, antisemitic conspiracy
theorist, Holocaust denier, convicted felon, and former Imperial Wizard of the
Ku Klux Klan.*

"I will be so good at the military your head will spin."

"Black entertainers love Donald Trump. Russell Simmons told me that."

"I don't care how sick you are. I don't care if you just came back from the doctor and he gave you the worst possible prognosis, meaning it's over. Doesn't matter. Hang out till November 8. Get out and vote."

"Did Crooked Hillary help disgusting (check out sex tape and past) Alicia M become a U.S. citizen so she could use her in the debate?"

On former Miss Universe Alicia Machado, who accused Trump of abuse

"I moved on her and I failed. I'll admit it. I did try and fuck her. She was married."

From a recording of Trump talking about TV host Nancy O'Dell on the set of Access Hollywood

"And I moved on her very heavily. In fact, I took her out furniture shopping. She wanted to get some furniture. I said, 'I'll show you where they have some nice furniture.'"

From a recording of Trump talking about TV host Nancy O'Dell on the set of Access Hollywood

"I moved on her like a bitch, but I couldn't get there. And she was married. Then all of a sudden I see her, she's now got the big phony tits and everything. She's totally changed her look."

From a recording of Trump talking about TV host Nancy O'Dell on the set of Access Hollywood

"I've gotta use some Tic Tacs, just in case I start kissing her. You know I'm automatically attracted to beautiful — I just start kissing them. It's like a magnet. Just kiss. I don't even wait. And when you're a star they let you do it. You can do anything."

From a recording of Trump talking on the set of Access Hollywood

"Grab them by the pussy. You can do anything."

From a recording of Trump talking on the set of Access Hollywood

"Oh, nice legs, huh?"

From a recording of Trump talking on the set of Access Hollywood

"It's just words, folks. Just words."

Referring to his insults and attacks

"If I win I'm going to instruct the attorney general to get a special prosecutor to look into your situation because there's never been so many lies, so much deception. [W]e're going to get a special prosecutor because people have been, their lives have been destroyed for doing one fifth of what you've done."

To presidential rival Hillary Clinton during a debate

"So this year, we have an election coming up on November 8, so important that you get out and vote. So important that — watch other communities because we don't want this election stolen from us. We do not want this election stolen from us."

"I'd look her right in that fat, ugly face of hers. She's a slob. She ate like a pig."

From a campaign ad run by the Clinton campaign, using Trump's own quotes and voice.

"...tremendous hate in her heart... she's got tremendous hatred..."

Referring to presidential rival Hillary Clinton

"No, you're the puppet. YOU ARE."

After being accused by presidential rival Hillary Clinton of being a puppet of Russian leader Vladimir Putin

"Such a nasty woman..."

To presidential rival Hillary Clinton during a presidential debate

"Nobody has more respect for women than me. Nobody."

"It is so nice that the shackles have been taken off me and I can now fight for America the way I want to."

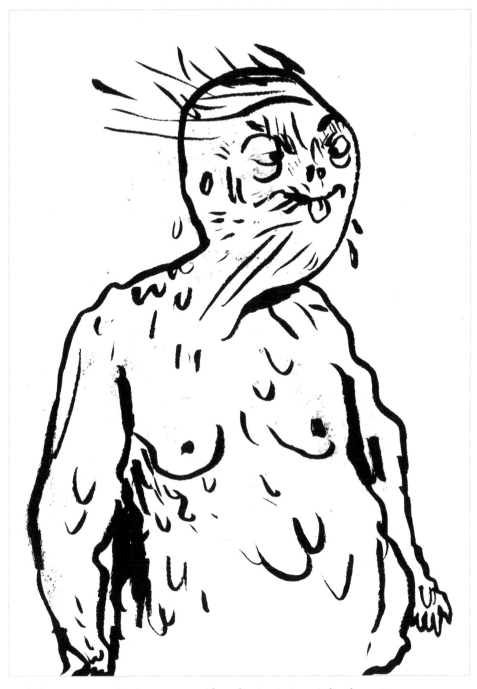

"I didn't even apologize to my wife, who is sitting right there."

Referring to sexual assault claims against Trump

"As everybody knows, but the haters & losers refuse to acknowledge, I do not wear a 'wig.' My hair may not be perfect but it's mine."

"Because you'd be in jail."

To Hillary Clinton during a presidential debate:

"And I consider myself, in a certain way, to be a blue-collar worker."

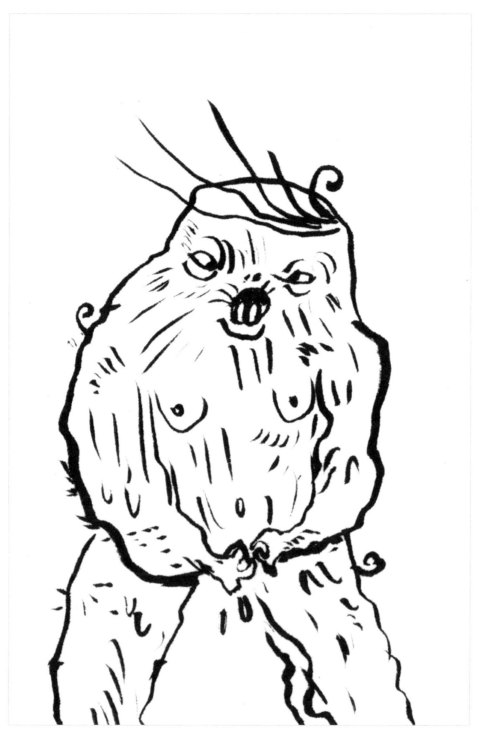

"...we have some bad hombres here and we're going to get them out."

"What I'm saying is I'll tell you at the time. I'll keep you in suspense, OK?"

On whether he would accept the election results if he lost

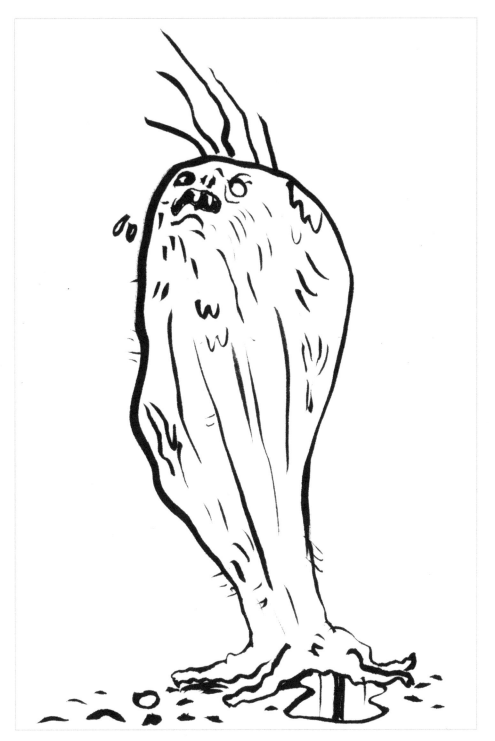

"And we're going to work on our, the ghettos – are in, so, the, you take a look at what's going on where you have pockets of, areas of land where you have the inner cities, and you have so many things, so many problems."

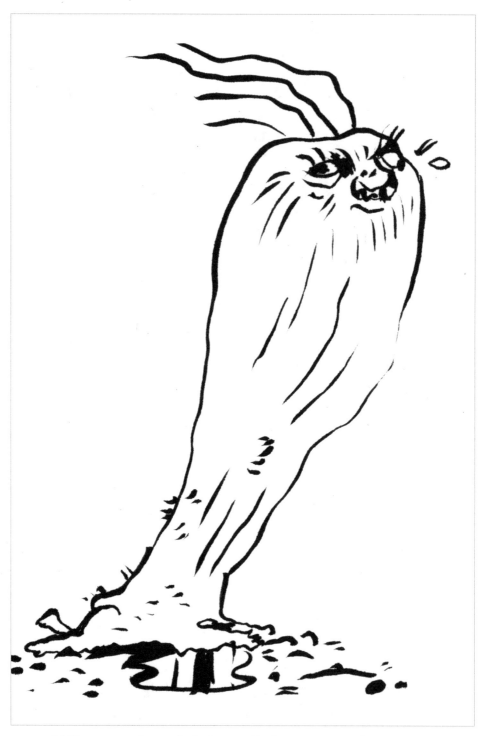

"I would like to promise and pledge to all of my voters and supporters and to all of the people of the United States that I will totally accept the results of this great and historic presidential election. If I win."

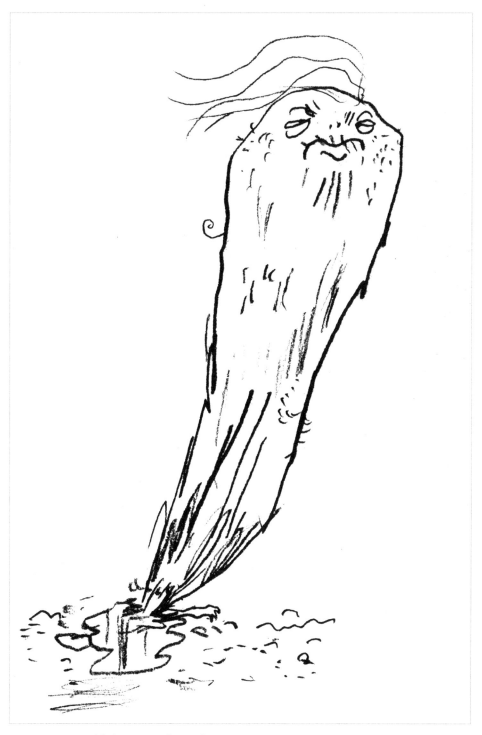

"Were you paid $1,500 to be a thug?"

To an African-American supporter

"She's a very low-energy person."

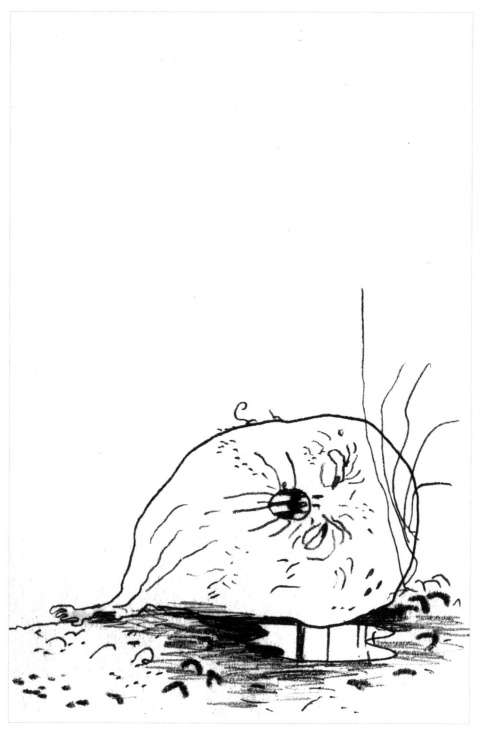

"You can tell your military expert that I'll sit down and I'll teach him a couple of things..."

"Do you think Bill was referring to Hillary when he said, 'I did not have sex with that woman'?"

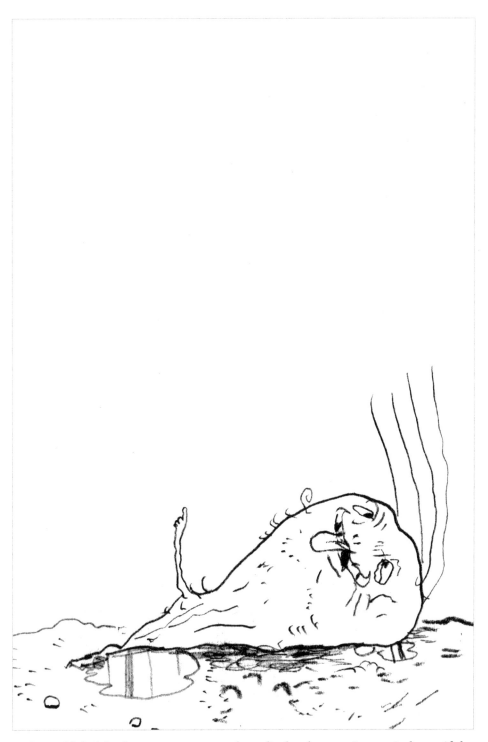

"A beautiful girl who was 17 or 18 and applied to be a waitress. So beautiful. She's like a world-class beauty. So I interviewed her anyway because she was so pretty. And I said, 'Let me ask you: Do you have any experience?' She goes, 'No, sir.' I say, 'When can you start?'"

"I'm asking you to dream big."

"I'm brave in other ways — I'm financially brave. Big deal."

"Is there any place more fun to be than a Trump rally?"

"Make America great again."

Election Day

"... I'm reaching out to you for your guidance and your help so that we can work together and unify our great country."

"The Electoral College is a disaster for a democracy."

"Just had a very open and successful presidential election. Now professional protesters, incited by the media, are protesting. Very unfair!"

Next day:

"Love the fact that the small groups of protesters last night have passion for our great country. We will all come together and be proud!"

"I have a lot of first priorities."

"We're going to get to work immediately for the American people."

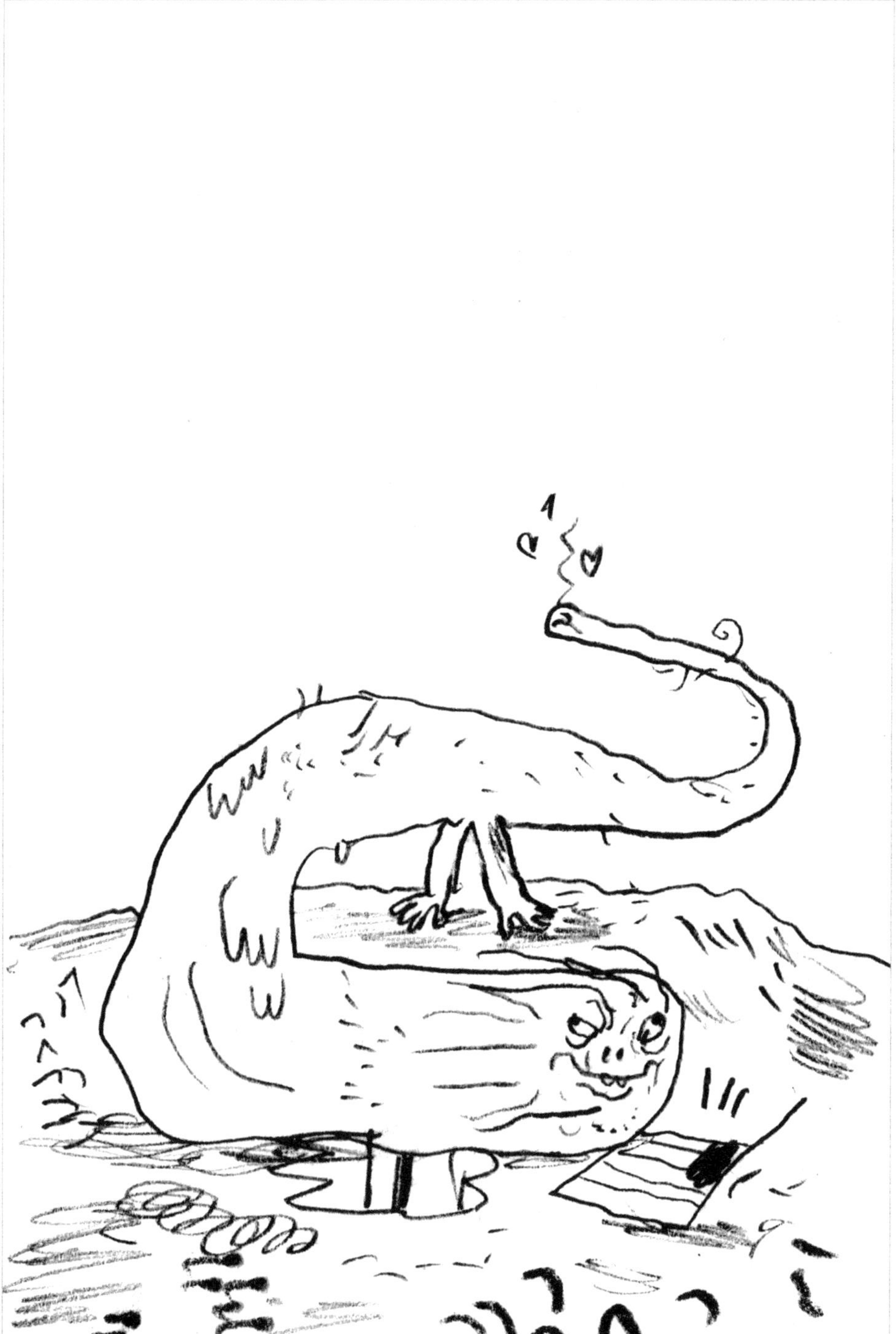

"It's going to happen."

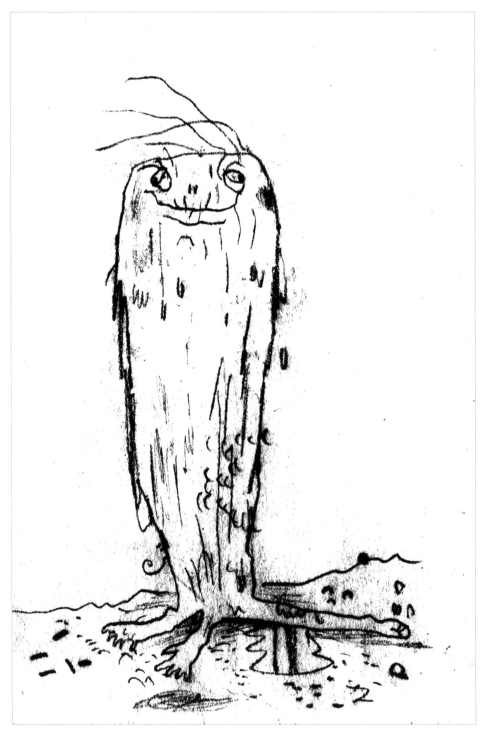

"Given the opportunity, I will get even with people who are disloyal to me."

"Don't be afraid. We are going to bring our country back. But certainly, don't be afraid."

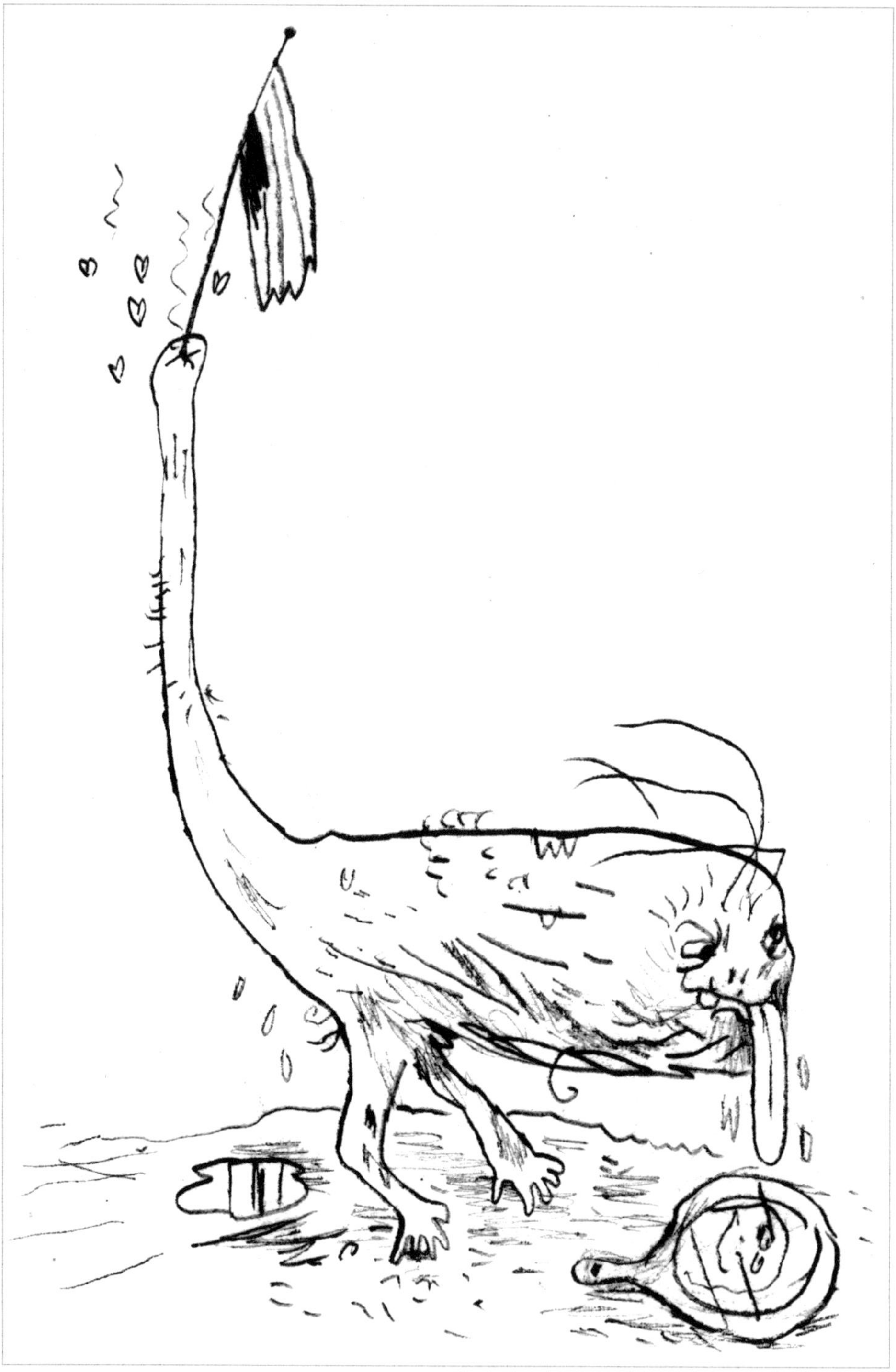

“I respect the FBI a lot.”

"When the economy crashes, when the country goes to total hell and everything is a disaster. Then you'll have a [chuckles], you know, you'll have riots to go back to where we used to be when we were great."

"The Theater must always be a safe and special place. The cast of Hamilton was very rude last night to a very good man, Mike Pence. Apologize!"

"Our wonderful future V.P. Mike Pence was harassed last night at the theater by the cast of Hamilton, cameras blazing. This should not happen!"

"I've done a lotta big things, I've never done anything like this. It is so big, it is so – it's so enormous, it's so amazing."

"Just got a call from my friend Bill Ford, Chairman of Ford, who advised me that he will be keeping the Lincoln plant in Kentucky - no Mexico"

"I worked hard with Bill Ford to keep the Lincoln plant in Kentucky. I owed it to the great State of Kentucky for their confidence in me!"

"I settled the Trump University lawsuit for a small fraction of the potential award because as President I have to focus on our country."

Soon after the election Trump paid $25 million to settle a fraud lawsuit related to "Trump University."

"The ONLY bad thing about winning the Presidency is that I did not have the time to go through a long but winning trial on Trump U. Too bad!"

"I can turn anyone into a successful real estate investor, including you."

"The law's totally on my side, the president can't have a conflict of interest."

"Prior to the election it was well known that I have interests in properties all over the world. Only the crooked media makes this a big deal!"

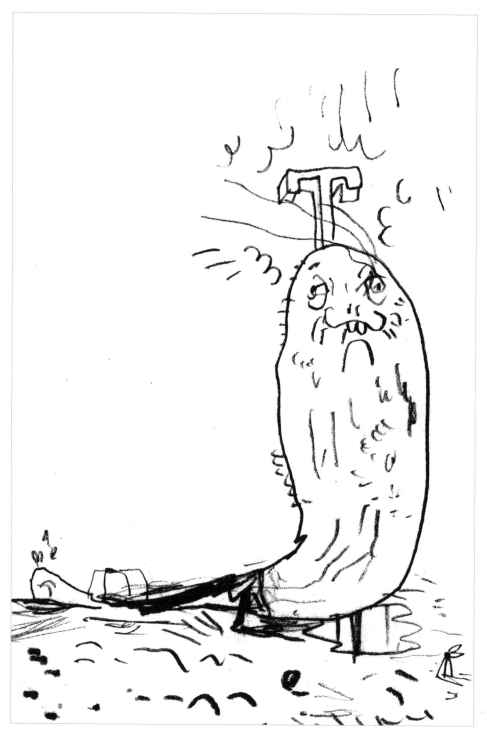

"In addition to winning the Electoral College in a landslide, I won the popular vote if you deduct the millions of people who voted illegally"

"This will prove to be a great time in the lives of ALL Americans. We will unite and we will win, win, win!"

"Great meetings will take place today at Trump Tower concerning the formation of the people who will run our government for the next 8 years."

"Well, sometimes you need a certain rhetoric to get people motivated."

"I've known Steve Bannon a long time. If I thought he was a racist or alt-right or any of the things, the terms we could use, I wouldn't even think about hiring him..."

Steve Bannon turned Breitbart News into a haven for "alt-right" anti-immigrant and white nationalist racists. Speaking about Breitbart, Bannon said, "We're the platform for the alt-right." He said that white nationalist racists are an "eclectic mix of renegades."

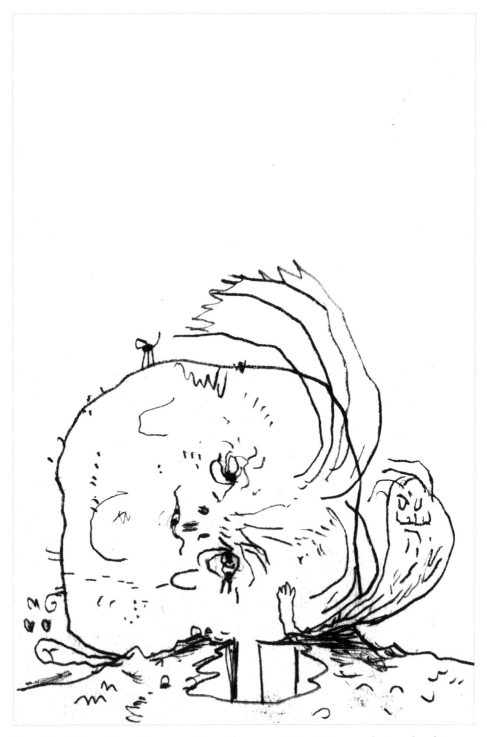

Trump advisor Steve Bannon: "Are there anti-Semitic people involved in the alt-right? Absolutely. Are there racist people involved in the alt-right? Absolutely. But I don't believe that the movement overall is anti-Semitic."

Some Breitbart News headlines published while it was under Trump advisor Steve Bannon's editorship:

Bill Kristol: Republican Spoiler, Renegade Jew

There's No Hiring Bias Against Women in Tech, They Just Suck at Interviews

Planned Parenthood's Body Count Under Cecile Richards is up to Half a Holocaust

Birth Control Makes Women Unattractive and Crazy

The Solution to Online 'Harassment' is Easy: Women Should Log Off

Trump advisor Steve Bannon: "That's why there are some unintended consequences of the women's liberation movement. That, in fact, the women that would lead this country would be pro-family, they would have husbands, they would love their children. They wouldn't be a bunch of dykes that came from the Seven Sisters schools up in New England."

Trump advisor Steve Bannon: "I'm a Leninist. Lenin wanted to destroy the state, and that's my goal too. I want to bring everything crashing down, and destroy all of today's establishment."

"Mike Pence is a man of honor, character and honesty."

As Indiana Governor, VP Elect Pence signed a 2015 bill allowing business owners to cite religious beliefs as a reason to refuse service to gay and lesbian customers.

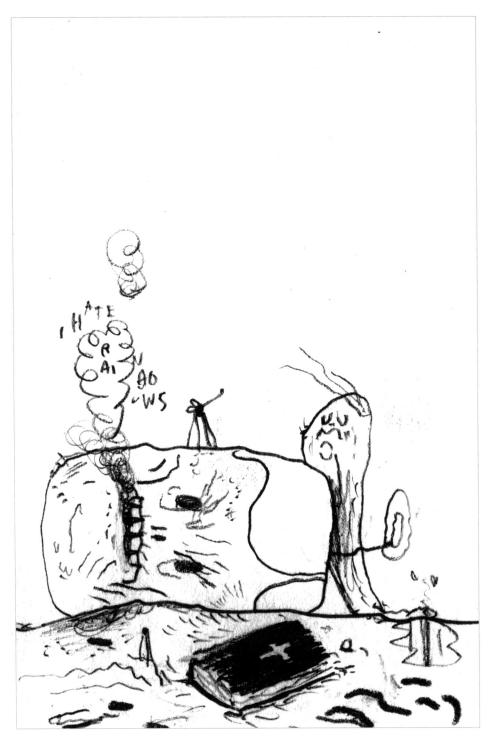

While in Congress, VP Elect Mike Pence cosponsored a bill that would have prohibited federal funds from paying for abortion except in cases of "forcible rape." As Governor of Indiana, Pence signed a bill into law requiring burial or cremation for aborted fetuses.

VP Elect Mike Pence wrote an op-ed arguing that "smoking doesn't kill."

As Governor of Indiana, VP Elect Mike Pence sought to create a taxpayer-funded state news outlet called "Just IN" that would have its own editorial and news teams, in hopes of creating a news service "overseen by political staff" that "could write stories that would be picked up by smaller newspapers that don't have big newsrooms." Pence eventually abandoned the plan after it was widely mocked as an attempt to create a Pravda-style propaganda outlet.

VP Elect Mike Pence wrote that the Disney movie "Mulan" justifies bans on women in combat since "young Ms. Mulan falls in love with her superior officer!" Pence writes, "You see, now stay with me on this, many young men find many young women to be attractive sexually. Many young women find many young men to be attractive sexually. Put them together, in close quarters, for long periods of time, and things will get interesting. Just like they eventually did for young Mulan. Moral of story: women in military, bad idea."

VP Elect Mike Pence:
- Signed a bill to jail same-sex couples for applying for a marriage license
- Tried to divert funding from HIV prevention to conversion therapy
- Urged Congress to "oppose any effort to recognize homosexual's [sic] as
  a 'discreet and insular minority' entitled to the protection of
  anti-discrimination laws"
- Urged Congress to "oppose any effort to put gay and lesbian relationships
  on an equal legal status with heterosexual marriage."

"Russia, if you're listening, I hope you're able to find the 30,000 emails that are missing. I think you will probably be rewarded mightily by our press."

Trump during the election, referring to Hillary Clinton's emails. He made this comment soon after his son, son-in-law and campaign manager met with a Russian agent about acquiring opposition research about Clinton.

CLINTON: Well, that's because he'd rather have a puppet as president of the United States.

TRUMP: No puppet. No puppet.

CLINTON: And it's pretty clear...

TRUMP: You're the puppet!

CLINTON: It's pretty clear you won't admit...

TRUMP: No, you're the puppet.

Third Presidential Debate, October 19, 2016

"Can you imagine if the election results were the opposite and WE tried to play the Russia/CIA card. It would be called conspiracy theory!"

"Unless you catch 'hackers' in the act, it is very hard to determine who was doing the hacking. Why wasn't this brought up before election?"

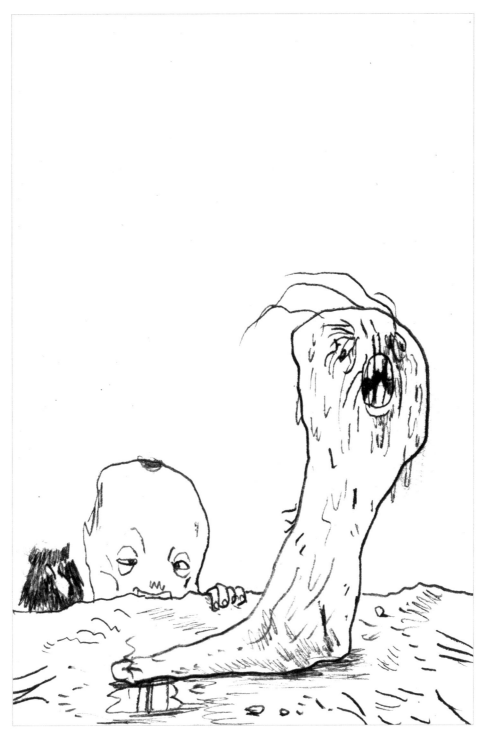

"I'm not going to tell Putin what to do. Why would I tell him what to do? ... Why do I have to get tough on Putin?"

"I think he respects me. I think it would be great to get along with him."

Trump about Putin

"It is always a great honor to be so nicely complimented by a man so highly respected within his own country and beyond."

Trump about Putin

"Will he become my new best friend?"

Trump about Putin

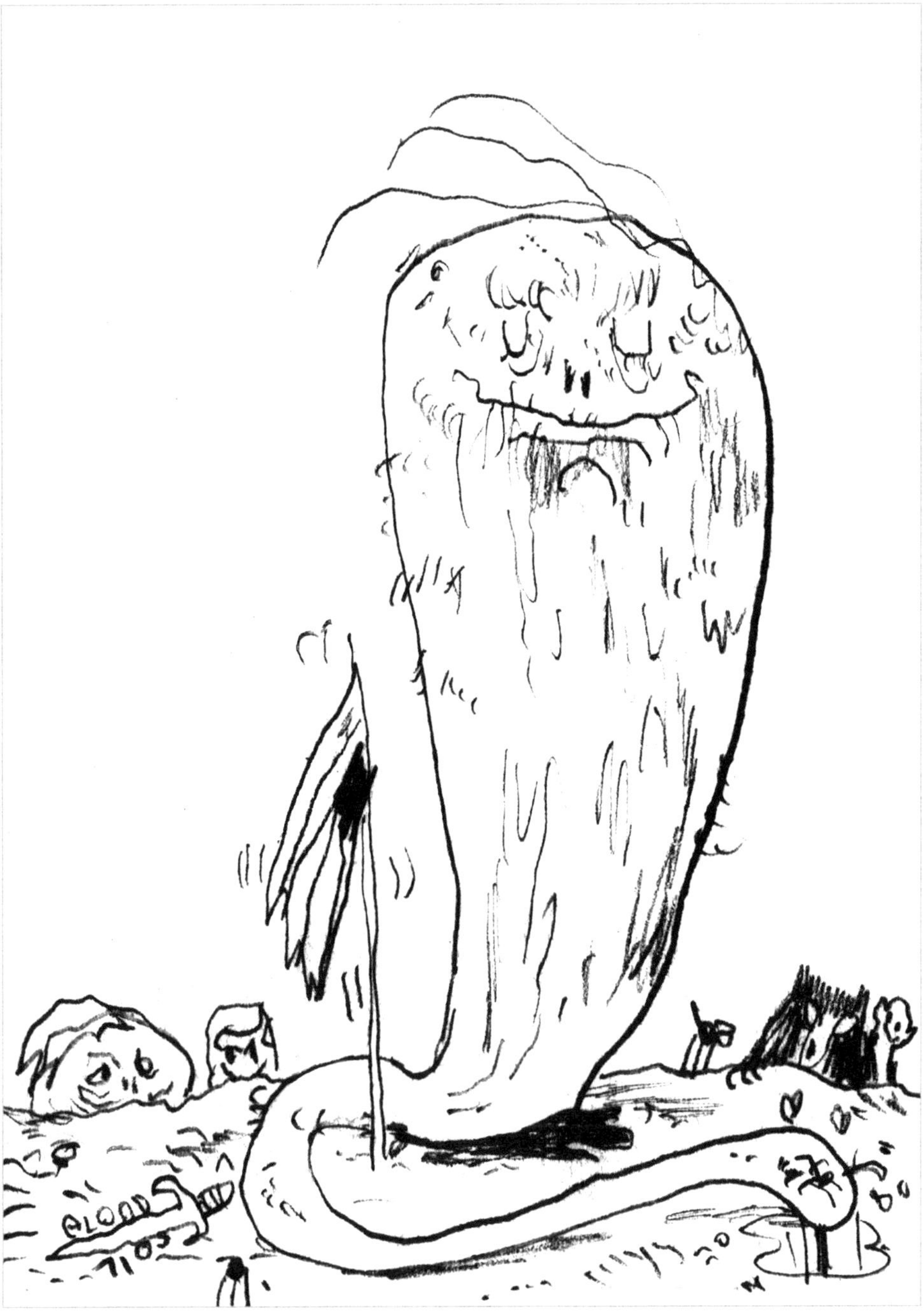
BLOOD
SOIL

"We did it! Thank you to all of my great supporters, we just officially won the election (despite all of the distorted and inaccurate media)."

The Electoral College submits final votes, confirming Trump's win.

"Reince is a superstar. But I said, "'They can't call you a superstar, Reince, unless we win,' because you can't be called a superstar — like Secretariat — if Secretariat came in second, Secretariat would not have that big, beautiful bronze bust at the track at Belmont. But I'll tell you, Reince is really a star. And he is the hardest-working guy. And in a certain way, I did this — Reince, come up here. Where is Reince? Get over here, Reince."

Trump on former RNC chair and future Trump chief of staff Reince Priebus

"It's possible."

Reince Priebus' answer when asked if Trump was correct when he said, without evidence, that millions of people had voted illegally

Trump Chief of Staff Reince Preibus: "People assume, oh, are you – you must be miserable. You've got a horrible job. But I don't see it that way. I'm not pouring Baileys in my cereal, I'm not sitting here trying to find a Johnnie Walker."

"I will go so strongly against so many of the things, when they take away the word 'Christmas.'"

"I'll tell you one thing: I get elected president, we're going to be saying 'Merry Christmas' again. Just remember that. And by the way, Christianity will have power, without having to form. Because if I'm there, you're going to have plenty of power. You don't need anybody else. You're going to have somebody representing you very, very well. Remember that."

"I'm a good Christian. If I become president, we're gonna be saying 'Merry Christmas' at every store ... You can leave 'Happy Holidays' at the corner."

"Merry Christmas and Happy Holidays" - Trump card, December 2015

Trump secretary of education nominee Betsy DeVos is an heiress who has championed the movement to privatize public education. She has worked to create programs and pass laws that require the use of public funds to pay for private school tuition, especially religious schools. DeVos has no personal experience with public education - she has never taught or administered one, and did not send her children to public schools.

Trump secretary of education nominee Betsy DeVos: "[M]y family is the largest single contributor of soft money to the national Republican party. ...I have decided, however, to stop taking offense at the suggestion that we are buying influence. Now, I simply concede the point. We expect to foster a conservative governing philosophy consisting of limited government and respect for traditional American virtues. We expect a return on our investment..."

Trump advisor Michael Flynn and his family repeatedly push bizarre conspiracy theories. His son tweeted: "Until #Pizzagate proven to be false, it'll remain a story. The left seems to forget #PodestaEmails and the many "coincidences" tied to it...."

Trump advisor Michael Flynn: "Fear of Muslims is RATIONAL."

"Doing my best to disregard the many inflammatory President O statements and roadblocks. Thought it was going to be a smooth transition - NOT!"

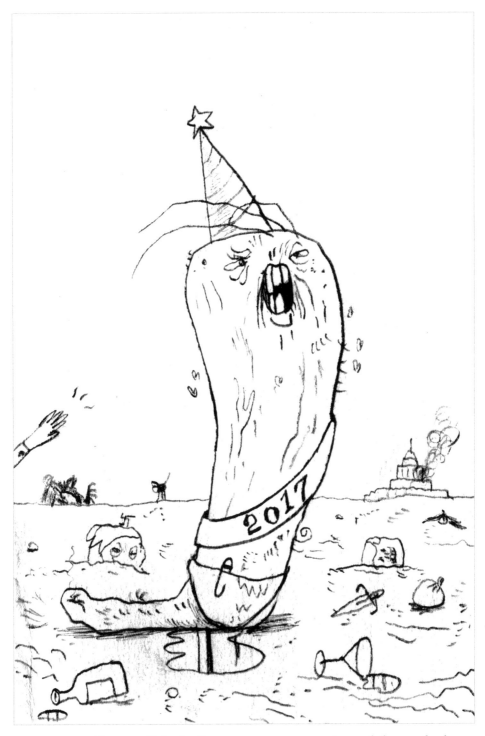

"Happy New Year to all, including to my many enemies and those who have fought me and lost so badly they just don't know what to do. Love!"

"TO ALL AMERICANS - #HappyNewYear & many blessings to you all!
Looking forward to a wonderful & prosperous 2017 as we work together to
#MAGA"

"The world was gloomy before I won - there was no hope. Now the market is up nearly 10% and Christmas spending is over a trillion dollars!"

"And I know a lot about hacking. And hacking is a very hard thing to prove. So it could be somebody else. And I also know things that other people don't know, and so they cannot be sure of the situation... You'll find out on Tuesday or Wednesday."

"I don't care what they say, no computer is safe. I have a boy who's 10 years old; he can do anything with a computer. You want something to really go without detection, write it out and have it sent by courier."

"With Ben Carson wanting to hit his mother on head with a hammer, stab a friend and Pyramids built for grain storage - don't people get it?"

Trump on his nominee for Department of Housing and Urban Development

Ben Carson, Trump's nominee for Department of Housing and Urban Development: "Obamacare is really I think the worst thing that has happened in this nation since slavery. And it is in a way, it is slavery in a way, because it is making all of us subservient to the government, and it was never about health care. It was about control."

Ben Carson, Trump's nominee for Department of Housing and Urban Development: "My own personal theory is that Joseph built the pyramids to store grain. Now all the archaeologists think that they were made for the pharaohs' graves. But, you know, it would have to be something awfully big if you stop and think about it. And I don't think it'd just disappear over the course of time to store that much grain."

"The DJT Foundation, unlike most foundations, never paid fees, rent, salaries or any expenses. 100% of money goes to wonderful charities!"

"I gave millions of dollars to DJT Foundation, raised or recieved millions more, ALL of which is given to charity, and media won't report!"

"The United States must greatly strengthen and expand its nuclear capability until such time as the world comes to its senses regarding nukes"

Trumps nominee for attorney general, Jefferson Beauregard "Jeff" Sessions III* was earlier denied a post as a judge because of his racist past.

A black assistant U.S. attorney who worked under Sessions testified that Sessions said he thought the Ku Klux Klan was okay until he learned its members smoked marijuana. Sessions told him to "be careful what you say to white folks."

Another Justice Department lawyer heard Sessions talk about his view of black civil rights groups, calling the NAACP a "commie pinko organization."

*Named after the president and a general from the Confederacy.

From Jeff Session's attorney general confirmation hearings:
SEN. WHITEHOUSE: And a secular person has just as good a claim to understanding the truth as a person who is religious, correct?
SESSIONS: Well, I'm not sure.

Trump attorney general nominee Jeff Sessions: "The Constitution says we shall not establish a religion — Congress shall not establish a religion. It doesn't say states couldn't establish a religion."

"FAKE NEWS - A TOTAL POLITICAL WITCH HUNT!"

"Intelligence agencies should never have allowed this fake news to "leak" into the public. One last shot at me.Are we living in Nazi Germany?"

A dossier allegedly compiled by a former British Intelligence officer, Christopher Steele, reportedly contains intelligence about Trump and his interactions with the Russian agents, including a night where he had Russian sex workers urinate on him and a bed that President Obama had slept in.

Trump secretary of state nominee Rex Tillerson, CEO of ExxonMobil, who has no diplomatic experience and has close personal and business ties to Russia and Vladimir Putin.

He argued against sanctions imposed after Russia invaded and annexed the Crimea. "I have a very close relationship with [Putin]." He claims ExxonMobil did not lobby against the sanctions when records show they did.

Trump's nominee for secretary of state, Rex Tillerson, who was awarded Russia's Order of Friendship by Vladimir Putin. From his nomination hearing:

SEN. MARCO RUBIO: "Is Vladimir Putin a war criminal?"

REX TILLERSON: "I would not use that term."

"Congressman John Lewis should spend more time on fixing and helping his district, which is in horrible shape and falling apart (not to mention crime infested) rather than falsely complaining about the election results. All talk, talk, talk - no action or results. Sad!"

One result John Lewis achieved as an activist was the Fair Housing Act of 1968, targeting racist landlords. Trump and his father were sued under this law.

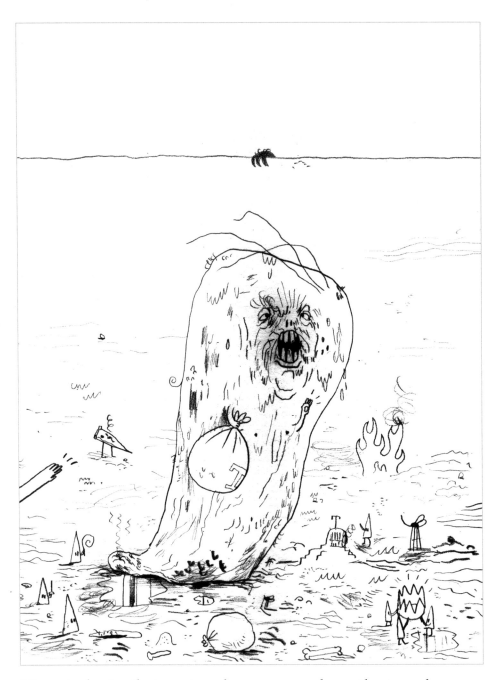

"I'm not releasing the tax returns because, as you know, they're under audit... The only one that cares about my tax returns are the reporters. They're the only ones."

"But I have a no conflict of interest provision as president. It was many, many years old, this is for presidents. Because they don't want presidents getting — I understand they don't want presidents getting tangled up in minutia; they want a president to run the country. So I could actually run my business, I could actually run my business and run government at the same time."

"The same people who did the phony election polls, and were so wrong, are now doing approval rating polls. They are rigged just like before."

"I look very much forward to the inauguration. It's going to be a beautiful event. We have great talent, tremendous talent. And we have all of the bands — or most of the bands from the different segments of the military. And I've heard some of these bands over the years — they're incredible. We're going to have a very, very elegant day."

"This is your day. This is your celebration. And this, the United States of America, is your country."

Inauguration Day.

LIVE DRAW OF THE INAUGURATION, JANUARY 20, 2017 *Originally posted on instagram*

Entering the Capitol

Some Trump kids

FLOTUS FOREVER

Jared and Ivanka

Melania

Obama and Diamond Joe

Waiting to walk out

Pence

Sigh.

Roy Blount

Prayer dude

Pretending to pray

some singing

Schumer bringing the heat!

Pence and Thomas

Sad Mormon choir

It has happened

Yuck

Ha ha it's raining

AMERICA FIRST

Trump people

This speech is unhinged

Ugh

More pray dudes

sadly singing the national anthem

OUR DEAR LEADER

Hillary and Bill

sad

Barack and Michelle

THANKS OBAMA. I mean that. I'll miss you

SOURCES AND NOTES

Pg 7 (07/21/16) http://www.marieclaire.co.uk/entertainment/people/donald-trump-quotes-57213

Pg 8 (07/22/16) https://www.washingtonpost.com/news/fact-checker/wp/2015/07/08/donald-trumps-false-comments-connecting-mexican-immigrants-and-crime/?utm_term=.504daed3eeee

Pg 9 (07/23/16) http://gawker.com/yet-another-bold-claim-from-donald-trump-i-know-words-1750331997

Pg 10 (07/24/16) https://www.youtube.com/watch?v=diMp241gAcw

Pg 11 (07/25/16) http://talkingpointsmemo.com/dc/trump-changes-few-minds-with-meeting-on-the-hill

Pg 12 (07/26/16) http://nypost.com/2011/04/03/trump-card/

Pg 13 (07/27/16) http://www.cbsnews.com/news/donald-trump-torture-works/

Pg 14 (07/28/16) http://www.cbsnews.com/pictures/wild-donald-trump-quotes/28/

Pg 15 (07/29/16) http://www.newsday.com/news/nation/donald-trump-speech-debates-and-campaign-quotes-1.11206532

Pg 16 (07/30/16) https://www.washingtonpost.com/politics/trumps-courtship-of-black-voters-hampered-by-decades-of-race-controversies/2016/07/19/d9822250-4d2e-11e6-aa14-e0c1087f7583_story.html?utm_term=.88c02953e8cb
This quote is from a memoir by former Trump associate John O'Donnell and is disputed.

Pg 17 (07/31/16) http://www.npr.org/2016/06/04/480714972/trump-presses-case-that-mexican-judge-curiel-is-biased-against-him

Pg 18 (08/01/16) http://www.newsday.com/news/nation/donald-trump-speech-debates-and-campaign-quotes-1.11206532

Pg 19 (08/02/16) http://www.independent.co.uk/news/world/americas/donald-trump-reiterates-desire-to-murder-terrorists-families-a6912496.html#gallery

Pg 20 (08/03/16) http://www.politico.com/blogs/2016-gop-primary-live-updates-and-results/2016/03/donald-trump-geneva-conventions-221394?cmpid=sf

Pg 21 (08/04/16) http://www.charlotteobserver.com/news/politics-government/article83831582.html

Pg 22 (08/05/16) http://www.newsday.com/news/nation/donald-trump-speech-debates-and-campaign-quotes-1.11206532

Pg 23 (08/06/16) http://www.independent.co.uk/news/world/americas/donald-trump-reiterates-desire-to-murder-terrorists-families-a6912496.html#gallery

Pg 24 (08/07/16) http://fortune.com/2016/04/24/trump-act-like-wife/

Pg 25 (08/08/16) http://www.cnn.com/2016/08/02/politics/donald-trump-ashburn-virginia-crying-baby/

Pg 26 (08/09/16) http://nymag.com/daily/intelligencer/2016/08/trump-asked-advisor-why-cant-we-use-nuclear-weapons.html

Pg 27 (08/10/16) http://www.politico.com/story/2016/08/trump-phony-polls-226567

Pg 28 (08/11/16) http://www.esquire.com/news-politics/politics/news/a47492/trump-hillary-assassination/

Pg 29 (08/12/16) http://abcnews.go.com/Politics/donald-trump-father-fallen-soldier-ive-made-lot/story?id=41015051

Pg 30 (08/13/16) http://www.newsmax.com/Newsfront/reince-priebus-donald-trump-rnc-republican/2016/08/11/id/743227/

Pg 31 (08/14/16) http://boingboing.net/2016/08/11/trump-says-barack-hussein.html

Pg 32 (08/15/16) http://abcnews.go.com/Politics/donald-trump-father-fallen-soldier-ive-made-lot/story?id=41015051

Pg 33 (08/16/16) http://fortune.com/2016/04/24/trump-act-like-wife/

Pg 34 (08/17/16) https://townhall.com/tipsheet/christinerousselle/2016/05/05/heres-donald-trumps-cinco-de-mayo-greeting-n2158612

Pg 35 (08/18/16) http://www.ibtimes.com/quotes-donald-trump-nato-what-republican-candidate-said-about-north-atlantic-treaty-2393661

Pg 36 (08/19/16) http://www.politico.com/story/2016/08/donald-trump-rigged-election-226588

Pg 37 (08/20/16) http://www.cnn.com/2015/12/02/politics/donald-trump-terrorists-families/index.html

Pg 38 (08/21/16) http://talkingpointsmemo.com/livewire/trump-no-need-get-out-the-vote

Pg 39 *(08/22/16)* http://www.philly.com/philly/news/politics/presidential/Donald_Trump_Hillary_Clinton_cheating_Pennsylvania_Altoona.html

Pg 40 *(08/23/16)* http://wjhl.com/2016/08/10/live-3pm-donald-trump-to-hold-rally-in-abingdon-va/

Pgs 41-54 *(08/24/16 - 09/06/16)* https://www.thoughtco.com/donald-trump-quotes-crazy-racist-idiot-2733864

Pg 55 *(09/07/16)* https://www.brainyquote.com/quotes/authors/d/donald_trump.html

Pg 56 *(09/08/16)* https://thedailybanter.com/2016/09/seven-quotes-donald-trump-will-want-to-forget-while-in-mexico/

Pg 57-58 *(09/09/16 - 09/10/16)* https://thedailybanter.com/2016/09/donald-trump-might-have-brain-damage/

Pg 59-63 *(09/11/16 - 09/15/16)* https://www.theguardian.com/us-news/2016/sep/08/trump-clinton-foreign-policy-forum-key-quotes

Pg 64-65 *(09/16/16 - 09/17/16)* https://thedailybanter.com/2016/09/seven-quotes-donald-trump-will-want-to-forget-while-in-mexico/

Pg 66 *(09/18/16)* http://www.cnn.com/2015/11/16/politics/donald-trump-paris-attacks-close-mosques/index.html

Pg 67 *(09/19/16)* https://www.nytimes.com/2016/09/17/us/politics/donald-trump-hillary-clinton.html

Pg 68 *(09/20/16)* http://www.latimes.com/politics/la-na-pol-trump-climate-miami-20160918-snap-story.html

Pg 69 *(09/21/16)* http://www.cnn.com/2016/09/09/politics/donald-trump-birther/index.html

Pg 70 *(09/22/16)* http://www.latimes.com/politics/la-na-pol-trump-climate-miami-20160918-snap-story.html

Pg 71 *(09/23/16)* http://www.businessinsider.com/donald-trump-business-philosophy-from-the-art-of-the-deal-2015-6

Pg 72 *(09/24/16)* http://www.golf.com/courses-and-travel/golf-magazine-interview-donald-trump

Pg 73 *(09/25/16)* http://www.thedailybeast.com/articles/2016/09/22/donald-trump-s-black-outreach-trainwreck-is-getting-worse-by-the-day

Pg 74 *(09/26/16)* http://fusion.kinja.com/the-collected-donald-trump-107-of-his-worst-weirdest-1793857006

Pg 75 *(09/27/16)* https://www.thoughtco.com/donald-trump-quotes-2733859

Pg 76 *(09/28/16)* https://www.usatoday.com/story/news/politics/onpolitics/2016/06/14/donald-trump-70-birthday-quotes/85619552/?siteID=je6NUbpObpQ-1PS_gz78if_4mE0zOWUDjg

Pg 77 *(09/29/16)* https://www.usatoday.com/story/news/politics/onpolitics/2016/06/14/donald-trump-70-birthday-quotes/85619552/?siteID=je6NUbpObpQ-NaURR0ILr.ipWEWWPxbJog
Full quote: "Look at my hands. ... My hands are normal hands. During a debate, he was losing, and he said, 'Oh, he has small hands and therefore, you know what that means.' This was not me. This was Rubio that said, 'He has small hands and you know what that means.' OK? So, he started it. So, what I said a couple of days later ... and what happened is, I was on line shaking hands with supporters, and one of the supporters got up and he said, 'Mr. Trump, you have strong hands. You have good-sized hands.' And then another one would say, 'You have great hands, Mr. Trump, I had no idea.' I said, 'What do you mean?' He said, 'I thought you were, like, deformed, and I thought you had small hands.' I had 50 people. ... I mean, people were writing, 'How are Mr. Trump's hands?' My hands are fine. You know, my hands are normal. Slightly large, actually. In fact, I buy a slightly smaller than large glove, OK?"

Pg 78-79 *(09/30/16 - 10/01/16)* https://www.thoughtco.com/donald-trump-quotes-2733859

Pg 80 *(10/02/16)* https://www.usatoday.com/story/news/politics/onpolitics/2016/06/14/donald-trump-70-birthday-quotes/85619552/?siteID=je6NUbpObpQ-Icaxhhp.X9JTj1nyYY_Bwg

Pg 81 *(10/03/16)* https://www.thoughtco.com/donald-trump-quotes-2733859

Pg 82-83 *(10/04/16 - 10/05/16)* http://fusion.kinja.com/the-collected-donald-trump-107-of-his-worst-weirdest-1793857006

Pg 84 *(10/06/16)* http://www.newsweek.com/trumps-urges-terminally-ill-hang-so-they-can-vote-him-506773

Pg 85 *(10/07/16)* http://www.businessinsider.com/donald-trump-alicia-machado-miss-universe-2016-9

Pg 86-91 *(10/08/16 - 10/13/16)* https://www.bustle.com/articles/188425-transcript-of-donald-trump-access-hollywood-host-billy-bush-talking-about-women-is-as-lewd

Pg 92-93 *(10/14/16 - 10/15/16)* http://www.slate.com/articles/news_and_politics/politics/2016/10/donald_trump_tells_hillary_clinton_you_d_be_in_jail.html

Pg 94 *(10/16/16)* http://www.slate.com/blogs/the_slatest/2016/10/10/donald_trump_again_pushes_conspiracy_theory_that_other_communities_trying.html

Pg 95 *(10/17/16)* https://www.nytimes.com/2016/10/06/us/politics/campaign-ads.html

Pg 96 *(10/18/16)* http://www.slate.com/articles/news_and_politics/politics/2016/10/donald_trump_has_gone_full_breitbart.html

Pg 97 *(10/19/16)* http://hellogiggles.com/donald-trump-quotes-debate/2/

Pg 98 *(10/20/16)* https://www.thecut.com/2016/10/the-best-tweets-on-trump-saying-such-a-nasty-woman.html

Pg 99 *(10/21/16)* http://heavy.com/news/2016/10/best-donald-trump-quotes-from-the-third-presidential-debate-funny-october-19-2016-what-did-say-hillary-clinton-emails-video/

Pg 100 *(10/22/16)* http://www.cnn.com/2016/10/11/politics/donald-trump-paul-ryan-tweets/

Pg 101 *(10/23/16)* http://heavy.com/news/2016/10/best-donald-trump-quotes-from-the-third-presidential-debate-funny-october-19-2016-what-did-say-hillary-clinton-emails-video/

Pg 102 *(10/24/16)* http://fusion.kinja.com/the-collected-donald-trump-107-of-his-worst-weirdest-1793857006

Pg 103 *(10/25/16)* http://www.slate.com/articles/news_and_politics/politics/2016/10/donald_trump_tells_hillary_clinton_you_d_be_in_jail.html

Pg 104 *(10/26/16)* https://twitter.com/AshleyRParker/status/785579936719306752

Pg 105 *(10/27/16)* http://heavy.com/news/2016/10/best-donald-trump-quotes-from-the-third-presidential-debate-funny-october-19-2016-what-did-say-hillary-clinton-emails-video/

Pg 106 *(10/28/16)* http://www.charlotteobserver.com/news/politics-government/election/article109318702.html

Pg 107 *(10/29/16)* http://www.dispatch.com/content/stories/local/2016/10/28/ohio-politics-now-trump-promises-work-on-ghettos.html

Pg 108 *(10/30/16)* http://www.newsday.com/news/nation/donald-trump-speech-debates-and-campaign-quotes-1.11206532

Pg 109 *(10/31/16)* http://www.huffingtonpost.com/entry/donald-trump-black-supporter-thug_us_58139e7ce4b064e1b4b253f2

Pg 110 *(11/01/16)* http://www.cbsnews.com/news/elections-2016-donald-trump-criticizes-coalition-mosul-iraq-take-back-from-isis/

Pg 111 *(11/02/16)* http://www.foxnews.com/politics/2016/10/27/trump-touts-new-deal-for-black-america-at-campaign-rally-in-charlotte.html

Pg 112 *(11/03/16)* https://www.nytimes.com/2016/11/05/us/politics/campaign-trump-clinton.html

Pg 113 *(11/04/16)* http://www.motherjones.com/politics/2016/09/watch-donald-trump-hire-woman-hot

Pg 114 *(11/05/16)* http://talkingpointsmemo.com/livewire/donald-trump-approaches-the-finish-line-as-unhinged-as-ever

Pg 115 *(11/06/16)* https://www.theguardian.com/us-news/live/2016/nov/03/donald-trump-hillary-clinton-melania-us-election-2016-news-live

Pg 116 *(11/07/16)* http://www.politico.com/story/2016/11/trump-speech-admires-mask-230883

Pg 117 *(11/08/16)* https://www.donaldjtrump.com

Pg 118 *(11/09/16)* https://www.nytimes.com/2016/11/10/us/politics/trump-speech-transcript.html

Pg 119-120 *(11/10/16 - 11/11/16)* https://twitter.com/realdonaldtrump

Pg 121 *(11/12/16)* https://www.wsj.com/articles/donald-trump-willing-to-keep-parts-of-health-law-1478895339

Pg 122-123 *(11/13/16 - 11/14/16)* https://www.nytimes.com/2016/11/10/us/politics/trump-speech-transcript.html

Pg 124 *(11/15/16)* https://www.youtube.com/watch?v=YDmxocrjuOo

Pg 125-126 *(11/16/16 - 11/17/16)* http://www.cbsnews.com/news/60-minutes-donald-trump-family-melania-ivanka-lesley-stahl/

Pg 127 *(11/18/16)* http://gothamist.com/2016/11/17/will_america_fire_itself.php

Pg 128 *(11/19/16)* http://www.cnn.com/2016/11/20/politics/donald-trump-hamilton-feud/index.html

Pg 129 *(11/20/16)* https://www.washingtonpost.com/news/the-fix/wp/2016/11/14/donald-trumps-first-tv-interview-since-getting-elected-president-shows-hes-not-going-to-change-much/?utm_term=.bd443a8cbee8

Pg 130 (11/21/16) https://www.nytimes.com/2016/11/18/us/politics/donald-trump-takes-credit-for-helping-to-save-a-ford-plant-that-wasnt-closing.html?_r=0

Pg 131-132 (11/22/16 - 11/23/16) https://twitter.com/realDonaldTrump

Pg 133 (11/24/16) http://www.newyorker.com/news/john-cassidy/trump-university-its-worse-than-you-think

Pg 134 (11/25/16) https://www.washingtonpost.com/blogs/plum-line/wp/2016/11/22/trump-may-have-just-flatly-and-openly-admitted-to-a-conflict-of-interest/?utm_term=.37a8c4c8409f

Pg 135 - 138 (11/26/16 - 11/29/16) https://twitter.com/realDonaldTrump

Pg 139 (11/30/16) http://www.cbsnews.com/news/60-minutes-donald-trump-family-melania-ivanka-lesley-stahl/

Pg 140-141 (12/01/16 - 12/02/16) **https://www.**theguardian.com/us-news/2016/nov/22/donald-trump-steve-bannon-alt-right-white-nationalist-**disavow and** http://www.motherjones.com/politics/2016/08/stephen-bannon-donald-trump-alt-right-breitbart-news

Pg 142 (12/03/16) https://www.mediamatters.org/blog/2016/08/17/breitbart-news-worst-headlines/212467

Pg 143 (12/04/16) https://www.buzzfeed.com/andrewkaczynski/trump-campaign-ceo-once-blasted-bunch-of-dykes-from-the-seve?utm_term=.fo8r3bRxXA#.emMZm18dWg

Pg 144 (12/05/16) http://www.thedailybeast.com/articles/2016/08/22/steve-bannon-trump-s-top-guy-told-me-he-was-a-leninist

Pg 145 (12/06/16) **https://www.lifesitenews.com/**news/trump-believes-pence-makes-sense-as-vp-choice and http://www.motherjones.com/politics/2016/10/mike-pence-isnt-boring-hes-one-americas-most-extreme-governors/

Pg 146-147 (12/07/16 - 12/08/16) **http://www.**rightwingwatch.org/post/a-dozen-reasons-why-mike-pence-is-just-as-bad-as-donald-trump/ and http://www.motherjones.com/politics/2016/10/mike-pence-isnt-boring-hes-one-americas-most-extreme-governors

Pg 148-149 (12/09/16 - 12/10/16) http://www.rightwingwatch.org/post/a-dozen-reasons-why-mike-pence-is-just-as-bad-as-donald-trump/

Pg 150 (12/11/16) https://www.lgbtqnation.com/2016/07/mike-pences-top-seven-homophobic-moments-many/

Pg 151 (12/12/16) https://www.nytimes.com/2016/07/28/us/politics/donald-trump-russia-clinton-emails.html

Pg 152 (12/13/16) https://www.nytimes.com/2016/10/20/us/politics/third-debate-transcript.html *Full transcript:*

CLINTON: Well, that's because he'd rather have a puppet as president of the United States.
TRUMP: No puppet. No puppet.
CLINTON: And it's pretty clear...
TRUMP: You're the puppet!
CLINTON: It's pretty clear you won't admit...
TRUMP: No, you're the puppet.
CLINTON: ... that the Russians have engaged in cyberattacks against the United States of America, that you encouraged espionage against our people, that you are willing to spout the Putin line, sign up for his wish list, break up NATO, do whatever he wants to do, and that you continue to get help from him, because he has a very clear favorite in this race.
So I think that this is such an unprecedented situation. We've never had a foreign government trying to interfere in our election. We have 17 — 17 intelligence agencies, civilian and military, who have all concluded that these espionage attacks, these cyberattacks, come from the highest levels of the Kremlin and they are designed to influence our election. I find that deeply disturbing.
WALLACE: Secretary Clinton...
CLINTON: And I think it's time you take a stand...
TRUMP: She has no idea whether it's Russia, China, or anybody else.
CLINTON: I am not quoting myself.
TRUMP: She has no idea.
CLINTON: I am quoting 17...
TRUMP: Hillary, you have no idea.
CLINTON: ... 17 intelligence — do you doubt 17 military and civilian...
TRUMP: And our country has no idea.
CLINTON: ... agencies.
TRUMP: Yeah, I doubt it. I doubt it.
CLINTON: Well, he'd rather believe Vladimir Putin than the military and civilian intelligence professionals who are sworn to protect us. I find that just absolutely...
(CROSSTALK)
TRUMP: She doesn't like Putin because Putin has outsmarted her at every step of the way.

Pg 153-154 (12/14/16 - 12/15/16) https://twitter.com/realDonaldTrump

Pg 155-158 (12/16/16 - 12/19/16) http://www.cnn.com/2016/07/28/politics/donald-trump-vladimir-putin-quotes/

Pg 159 (12/19/16) https://twitter.com/realdonaldtrump/status/810996052241293312?lang=en

Pg 160 (12/20/16) https://www.nytimes.com/2016/11/10/us/politics/trump-speech-transcript.html Full transcript:
"Reince is a superstar. But I said, "They can't call you a superstar, Reince, unless we win," because you can't be called a superstar — like Secretariat — if Secretariat came in second, Secretariat would

not have that big, beautiful bronze bust at the track at Belmont. But I'll tell you, Reince is really a star. And he is the hardest-working guy. And in a certain way, I did this — Reince, come up here. Where is Reince? Get over here, Reince."

Pg 161 (12/21/16) http://www.cbsnews.com/news/face-the-nation-transcript-december-4-2016-priebus-gingrich-pelosi-panetta/

Pg 162 (12/22/16) https://www.theguardian.com/us-news/2016/nov/14/who-are-trump-appointees-reince-priebus-and-stephen-bannon

Pg 163 (12/23/16) http://thepoliticalinsider.com/trump-just-made-huge-announcement-about-his-plans-for-the-word-christmas-shock/#ixzz4TacuknOLn

Pg 164 (12/24/16) http://www.businessinsider.com/donald-trump-christianity-merry-christmas-2016-1

Pg 165 (12/25/16) http://www.cnn.com/2015/10/21/politics/donald-trump-iowa-rally/ and http://www.express.co.uk/news/world/629343/Donald-Trump-Christmas-card-message-politically-correct

Pg 166 (12/26/16) https://www.washingtonpost.com/news/answer-sheet/wp/2016/12/08/a-sobering-look-at-what-betsy-devos-did-to-education-in-michigan-and-what-she-might-do-as-secretary-of-education/?utm_term=.d6d72d5b1a76

Pg 167 (12/27/16) http://www.sourcewatch.org/index.php/Betsy_DeVos

Pg 168 (12/28/16) http://www.politico.com/story/2016/12/michael-flynn-conspiracy-pizzeria-trump-232227

Pg 169 (12/29/16) https://www.nytimes.com/2016/11/19/opinion/michael-flynn-an-alarming-pick-for-national-security-adviser.html

Pg 170-173 (12/30/16 - 01/02/17) https://twitter.com/realDonaldTrump

Pg 174-175 (01/03/17 - 01/04/17) https://www.nytimes.com/2016/12/31/us/politics/donald-trump-russia-hacking.html?_r=0

Pg 176 (01/05/17) https://twitter.com/realdonaldtrump/status/662632599962173440?lang=en

Pg 177-178 (01/06/17 - 01/07/17) http://www.politico.com/story/2015/10/ben-carson-controversial-quotes-214614

Pg 179 (01/08/17) https://twitter.com/realdonaldtrump/status/813581917215977473?lang=en and https://twitter.com/realDonaldTrump/status/813578484572450816

Pg 180 (01/09/17) https://twitter.com/realdonaldtrump/status/811977223326625792?lang=en

Pg 181 (01/10/17) http://www.thedailybeast.com/articles/2017/01/09/jeff-sessions-wanted-to-drop-the-case-against-kkk-lynching-attorney-testified

Pg 182 (01/11/17) http://edition.cnn.com/TRANSCRIPTS/1701/10/cg.01.html

Pg 183 (01/12/17) https://www.nytimes.com/interactive/2017/01/08/us/politics/jeff-sessions-on-the-issues.html

Pg 184 (01/12/17) https://twitter.com/realdonaldtrump/status/818990655418617856?lang=en and https://twitter.com/realdonaldtrump/status/819164172781060096?lang=en

Pg 185 (01/13/17) http://money.cnn.com/2017/01/11/investing/tillerson-exxon-sanctions-russia-iran/ and https://www.bustle.com/articles/199835-rex-tillerson-quote-on-putin-acknowledges-very-close-relationship-with-the-russian-leader and https://en.wikipedia.org/wiki/Rex_Tillerson

Pg 186 (01/14/17) http://insider.foxnews.com/2017/01/11/putin-war-criminal-rubio-grills-rex-tillerson-secretary-state-russia-trump

Pg 187 (01/15/17) https://twitter.com/realdonaldtrump/status/820251730407473153?lang=en and https://twitter.com/realdonaldtrump/status/820255947956383744?lang=en and https://en.wikipedia.org/wiki/Fair_Housing_Act

Pg 188-189 (01/16/17 - 01/17/17) https://www.nytimes.com/2017/01/11/us/politics/trump-press-conference-transcript.html

Pg 190 (01/18/17) https://twitter.com/realdonaldtrump/status/821344302651555840?lang=en

Pg 191 (01/19/17) http://www.thewrap.com/11-memorable-quotes-from-wild-donald-trump-press-conference/

Pg 192 (01/20/17) https://www.whitehouse.gov/inaugural-address

Warren Craghead III lives in Charlottesville, Virginia, USA with his wife and two daughters.

He likes to make pictures and has exhibited his work internationally. He has also published many works including the Xeric Grant winning *Speedy* and several collaborations with poets and writers. He has been nominated for an Ignatz Award and a Pushcart Prize and is a three-time Virginia Museum of Fine Art Fellow.

He received an MFA in 1996 from the University of Texas at Austin, a BFA from Virginia Commonwealth University in Richmond, Virginia in 1993, and attended the Skowhegan School in 1993.

See his work at craghead.com.
See daily updates of Trump drawings at trumptrump.biz.

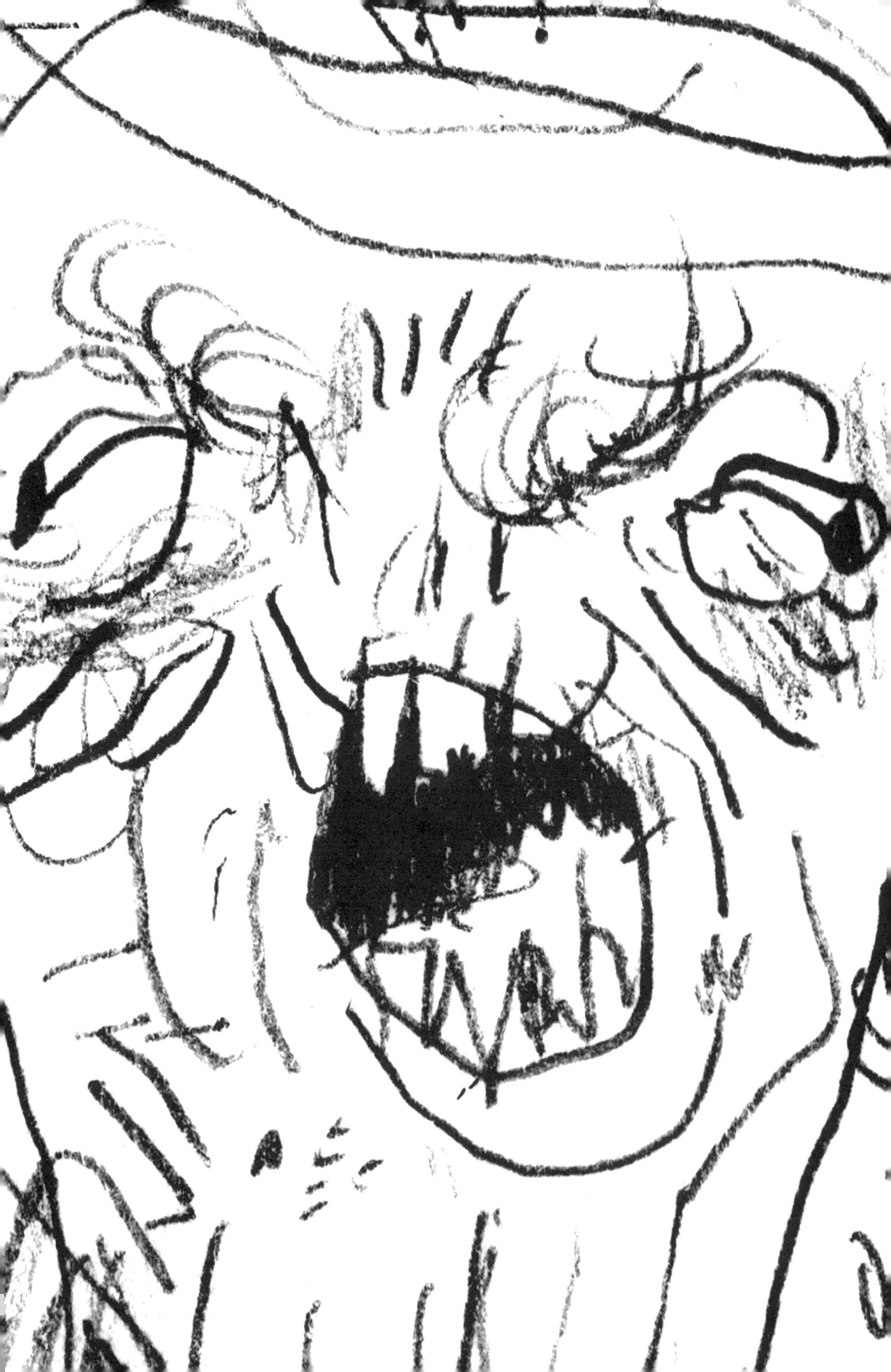